4 Weeks

of

Fabulous

Paleolithic

Lunches

by Amelia Simons

Other Books by Amelia Simons

Complete Paleo Meals: A Paleo Cookbook Featuring Paleo Comfort Foods

Gluten-Free Slow Cooker: Easy Recipes for a Gluten Free Diet

Paleo Slow Cooker Soups and Stews: Healthy Family Gluten-Free Recipes

Paleo Slow Cooker: Simple and Healthy Gluten-Free Recipes

Going Paleo: A Quick Start Guide for a Gluten-Free Diet

4 Weeks of Fabulous Paleolithic Breakfasts

4 MORE Weeks of Fabulous Paleolithic Breakfasts

4 Weeks of Fabulous Paleolithic Dinners

The Ultimate Paleolithic Collection

Table of Contents

A Little Taste of the Paleo Lifestyle

What is the Paleo lifestyle? The Paleolithic way of eating includes various names like: Primal Diet, Cave Man Diet, Stone Age Diet, Hunter-Gatherer Diet, and a few others. The Paleolithic lifestyle consists of a low-carb diet that attempts to imitate what our ancestors ate before farming and other advancements changed our diets.

As with many other ways of eating, there is some variation and degrees of limitations practiced by those who try to eat as our "primal" ancestors did. With that said, what follows are the basic guidelines that most proponents of the Paleolithic way of eating agree upon.

Whether or not you fully embrace this way of eating by going "cold turkey," or ease your way gently into the program, here are some basic guidelines.

What Foods Are Considered "Off Limits?"

Refined sugars: Basically, the rule is to avoid all sugars. These include white sugar, high fructose corn syrup, candy, milk chocolate, soda, and artificial sweeteners. Some spokespersons for Paleolithic allow small amounts of raw honey, pure maple syrup, and coconut sugar, but also advise these sugars to be an occasional treat.

Grains: The types of grain to avoid include wheat, rye, barley, rice, oats and corn. Foods would include bread, pasta, baked goods, pancakes, biscuits, muffins, bagels, and cereals. Grains are high in carbohydrates and are calorie-dense.

Legumes: This category includes beans of all kinds, peas, lentils, soybeans, tofu, soy products, and peanuts.

Dairy products: Try to exclude eating dairy products like regular milk, cream, fruit yogurts, ice cream, and processed cheeses.

- While many Paleo eaters eliminate dairy from their diet, others do not. If you can tolerate dairy and want to enjoy it on occasion, start with cultured butter, Greek yogurt (not fruit flavored), kefir, clotted milks, and aged cheeses. These are fermented products that drastically reduce the lactose (milk sugar) levels.

- Next would come raw, high-fat dairy like raw butter and cream because they are minimally processed and are good sources of saturated fat. Most of these are free from lactose and casein and should come from grass-fed, pasture-fed animals.

- Avoid homogenized and pasteurized milk. If you must buy it, make it organic, hormone and antibiotic-free milk. Because nuts are allowed, consider substituting unsweetened almond milk and coconut milk in place of cow's milk.

- Grass-fed butter is considered okay. If you want to eat cheese on occasion, too, be sure they are aged cheeses because aging drastically reduces the levels of lactose and casein.

Some meats: Avoid processed meats like hot dogs, bologna, and lunchmeats. If eating bacon and sausage, try to eat those without nitrates and nitrites. The bacon issue is still widely debated among the Paleo community—some believe it is okay if using nitrite/nitrate free bacon that is also sugar-free. Others believe because it is cured, it is not allowed. YOU DECIDE!

Oils: Avoid anything "partially hydrogenated," shortening, margarines, canola oil, soybean oil, cottonseed oil, peanut oil, corn oil, and sunflower oil. Note: be sure to check the label on your mayonnaise.

What Foods Are Allowed?

Meats, seafood and eggs: Meats, seafood, and eggs are perhaps the most important components of the Paleo Diet. These include beef, pork, lamb, bison, poultry, shrimp, crab, trout, salmon, mackerel, along with other wild-caught fish, including sardines, oysters, mussels, and clams. Once again, bacon and sausage is widely debated so you decide if it is okay for you or not.

Vegetables: Vegetables are greatly encouraged and can be eaten in unlimited quantities. Focus on leafy greens of all kinds. Whether or not to include potatoes and other starchy tubers in your diet is an area of varying opinions at this point.

Fruits: Fruits are allowed but should be limited, especially if you need to lose weight. High sugar fruits like dried fruits and juices should be eaten only occasionally.

Nuts and seeds: Nuts and seeds are allowed. They are high in fat so limit your intake if you want to lose weight. Nuts and seeds include macadamias, Brazil nuts, hazelnuts, pistachios, walnuts, almonds, pecans, cashews, squash seeds, sunflower seeds, and pumpkin seeds. **Note:** Peanuts are legumes and are not part of Paleolithic eating.

Healthy fats: Olive oil and nut oils like coconut oil are generally encouraged. Butter, palm oil, ghee, and animal fats are on the allowable list.

Beverages: All spokespersons agree that water is best and should be your main drink. Generally, tea is fine, while there continues to be some variations concerning coffee and alcohol. Beverages that require sweeteners by sugars or artificial sweeteners are discouraged.

Throughout this collection of recipes (and the others in my series), I have tried to guide you into this way of eating. The goal is to make positive changes toward this way of eating without making you feel like it has to be one certain way. Simply know your labels and use your best judgment.

If you cannot afford organic or grass-fed beef, do not fret about that. Just buy the basic ingredients and follow the basic guidelines for eating Paleolithic style.

I hope you enjoy this collection of Paleolithic recipes. These are some of my family's absolute favorites and I hope they become some of your favorites, too!

SALADS

Hearty Sautéed Peach Salad

Ingredients:

- 2 tablespoons coconut oil

- ¾ cup sliced peaches

- ½ cup grated carrots

- 1 cup chicken, cooked and shredded

- 1 teaspoon cinnamon

- 1 teaspoon nutmeg

- 3 cups fresh romaine lettuce, washed and broken into bite-sized pieces

Directions:

1. Heat the coconut oil in a saucepan over medium heat

2. Place the sliced peaches and grated carrots into the saucepan and sauté until tender

3. In a large bowl, place the chicken, cinnamon, and nutmeg

4. Now add the peaches and carrots into the bowl with the chicken and spices

5. Mix thoroughly

6. Add the romaine to the peach mixture and mix thoroughly

7. Add your favorite oil and vinegar dressing if desired

Broccoli & Bacon Salad

If you give yourself permission to eat bacon on occasion (like I do), you will truly enjoy the taste of this salad.

Ingredients:

- 8 ounce plain Greek yogurt or kefir (if you eat dairy)

- 1 egg

- 2 tablespoons vinegar

- 2 tablespoons raw honey

- 1 tablespoon olive oil

- 1 tablespoon mustard

- ¼ teaspoon sea salt

- ⅛ teaspoon garlic powder

- ⅛ teaspoon pepper

- 6 cups fresh broccoli, cut into bite size pieces

- ⅓ cups raisins (optional)

- 2 tablespoons chopped onions

- ½ pound bacon, cooked and crumbled (optional)

Directions:

1. Place the yogurt, egg, vinegar, honey, oil, mustard, salt, garlic powder, and pepper into your blender

2. Process the mixture until smooth

3. In a large mixing bowl, combine the broccoli, raisins, onions, and bacon.

4. Pour the sauce from the blender over the broccoli and mix thoroughly—until the broccoli is moist

5. Cover and place in the refrigerator until chilled

Grilled Taco Salad

Ingredients:

- 2 hearts of romaine lettuce, cut into quarters

- 1 onion, cut into chunks

- 1 green pepper, cut into chunks

- 2 tomatoes, cut into chunks

- 2 avocados, peeled, pitted, and cut in half

- 4 tablespoons olive oil

- ½ teaspoon cumin

- ¼ teaspoon paprika

- ¼ teaspoon chili powder

- ¼ teaspoon salt

- 1 pound skirt steak

Directions:

1. Turn your grill on to medium heat.

2. Take a large bowl and place the romaine quarters, onion, green pepper, tomatoes, and avocados into it.

3. Drizzle 2 tablespoons of olive oil over the vegetables and toss to coat.

4. Place the vegetables, including the romaine, into a grill basket or on skewers.

5. In a small bowl, mix the other 2 tablespoons of oil with the cumin, paprika, chili powder and salt.

6. Coat the steak with the spice mixture.

7. Place the steak onto the grill, along with the vegetables.

8. Close the lid and grill for 4 minutes.

9. After 4 minutes, flip the steak and grill basket to the other side.

10. Close the lid and grill for 4 more minutes.

11. After the steak is done to your liking, slice it and cut the romaine into bite-sized chunks.

12. Toss with the vegetables and add salt and pepper to taste.

Fruity Salad with Chicken

This recipe is fast and always delicious, especially if you already have some Paleo mayo made. If not, I have included a recipe for it here that you can make and keep in your refrigerator for the next time.

Ingredients:

- 12 ounces of canned white chicken

- 2 celery stalks, finely chopped

- ¼ cup chopped red onion

- ¼ cup Paleolithic mayonnaise (p. 16)

- ½ cup dried unsweetened cranberries

- ¼ cup chopped pecans (optional)

Directions:

1. In a medium-sized bowl, put the chicken, celery, onion, mayo cranberries and pecans (if desired).

2. Mix thoroughly.

3. Enjoy plain or make a wrap using lettuce leaves. I also like to use it as a dip with carrot chips, apple slices and even celery sticks.

How to Make Paleolithic Mayonnaise

Ingredients:

- 2 tablespoons freshly squeezed lemon juice

- 2 large eggs

- 1 teaspoon dry mustard

- Salt to taste. Start with 1 teaspoon

- 1/4 teaspoon cayenne pepper (optional)

- 2 cups olive oil

Directions:

1. In a blender, place the lemon juice, eggs, dry mustard, salt, and cayenne (if using)

2. Pulse for a few seconds until the mixture becomes frothy

3. Turn your blender on a low setting and allow it to keep running

4. Slowly add the oil—almost a drop at a time—to the mixture until it begins to emulsify

5. Keep adding the oil slowly until it is all blended in

6. Add salt to taste

7. Store in a container in your refrigerator

Asian Lobster Salad

Lobster is one of my favorite foods. I don't get to enjoy it very often, but when I do, this is a salad I like to make. This recipe is fun because you can also take your cabbage leaves (don't slice them like the recipe says to do), roll the lobster filling inside, and enjoy them as I've shown in the picture. Either way, it is delicious!

Ingredients:

- 1 pound cooked lobster meat

- 2 cups thinly sliced Napa cabbage

- ½ red bell pepper, thinly sliced

- 8 ounce can of water chestnuts, drained

- ½ cup fresh parsley, chopped

- ¼ cup slivered almonds, toasted

Dressing:

- 2 tablespoons chicken broth

- 2 tablespoons coconut aminos

- 1 tablespoon olive oil

- 1 teaspoon sesame oil

- 1 teaspoon fresh ginger, grated

Directions:

1. Cut the lobster meat into bite-sized pieces.

2. Place the cabbage, bell pepper, water chestnuts, parsley, and almonds into a medium bowl.

3. Mix ingredients thoroughly.

4. In a small bowl, whisk together the broth, aminos, olive oil, sesame oil, and ginger.

5. Pour dressing over salad.

6. Toss gently to coat.

Warm Shrimp Salad

Ingredients:

- Juice of 3 lemons

- 3 tablespoons raw honey

- 1 teaspoon minced garlic

- Salt & pepper to taste

- 2 tablespoons olive oil

- ½ pound large raw shrimp, peeled and cleaned

- ¼ teaspoon fresh ginger, finely grated

- ½ cup snap peas, diced

- 2 medium sized zucchini, diced

- ½ cup broccoli sprouts

- 2 tablespoons toasted sesame seeds (optional)

Directions:

1. In a small bowl, whisk together the lemon juice, honey, garlic, salt and pepper.

2. Pour half of the mixture over the shrimp, allowing it to marinate for a few minutes.

3. Heat the olive oil in a large skillet over medium-high heat.

4. Once hot, add the shrimp to the skillet and sauté until pink and cooked through.

5. In a medium bowl, combine the ginger, snap peas, zucchini, and sprouts.

6. Toss the warm, cooked shrimp into the bowl.

7. Toss with the remaining half of the lemon juice mixture and sesame seeds.

8. Serve immediately.

Note: A nice variation is to add in a few chunks of fresh pineapple if you have it. It isn't necessary, but it adds a whole new dimension.

Poached Egg Salad

Ingredients

- 4 eggs

- 3 tablespoons lemon juice

- 2 teaspoons Dijon mustard

- ¾ teaspoon sea salt

- ½ teaspoon fresh ground pepper

- ½ cup olive oil

- 4 ounces lean ground beef

- 6 cups mixed greens

- 4 ounces aged shredded cheddar cheese, (optional)

Directions

1. Poach eggs in an egg poacher, saucepan or microwave.

2. Cook until the egg whites are set but the yolks are still runny—about 4 minutes in an egg poacher or 2 minutes in the microwave.

3. To make the dressing, combine the lemon juice, mustard, salt and pepper in a blender.

4. Pour into a medium bowl and slowly whisk in the olive oil until the dressing thickens.

5. Set aside.

6. Place a frying pan over medium heat, sauté the beef until browned.

7. Toss the mixed greens with the dressing.

8. Sprinkle with the ground beef and shredded cheese.

9. Finally, place one egg on top of each serving of salad.

SOUPS

Cabbage and Beef Soup

I really enjoy soups all year round and this is one that is delicious and warms me through and through. Plus, with all the good foods in this one, it is quite nutritious as well.

Ingredients:

- ½ pound stewing beef

- 3 quarts water

- 2 bay leaves

- 1 small head of cabbage

- 4 large carrots, sliced

- 4 stalks of celery, chopped

- 1 large onion, diced

- 15 ounce can diced tomatoes

- 8 ounces 100% tomato juice

Directions:
1. Place the beef into a large pot and fill with 3 quarts of water.

2. Add the bay leaves.

3. Cover the pot and simmer for 3 hours to make sure the beef is tender.

4. Chop the cabbage, carrots, celery and onion.

5. Now add the vegetables to the pot with the beef. Cook for an additional 30 minutes.

6. Remove the bay leaves and add the tomatoes and the tomato juice.

7. Bring to a boil again and serve.

Note: If you wish, you can add in the tomatoes and tomato juice when you add in the other vegetables, too.

Sweet Potato Soup

Ingredients:

- 1 tablespoon coconut flour

- 1 tablespoon coconut oil

- 1½ cups chicken broth

- 1½ cups cooked cubed sweet potatoes

- ¼ teaspoon ground ginger (or fresh, to taste)

- ⅛ teaspoon ground cinnamon

- ⅛ teaspoon ground nutmeg

- 1 cup coconut milk

- Salt and pepper to taste

Directions:

1. In a saucepan over medium-low heat, cook the coconut flour and coconut oil, stirring constantly until the mixture turns a light caramel color.

2. Add the chicken broth and bring it to a boil.

3. Turn the heat down to low and then stir in the sweet potatoes, ginger, cinnamon, and nutmeg.

4. Cook on low for 5 more minutes and blend thoroughly.

5. Remove from the pot and place the mixture into a blender.

6. Puree the soup.

7. Now return to the saucepan.

8. Now add the coconut milk and gently reheat the soup.

9. Season with salt and pepper and serve.

Easy Vegetable Soup

Ingredients:

- 2 tablespoons coconut oil

- ¼ cup diced onion

- 1 cup thinly sliced carrots

- 1 cup thinly sliced zucchini

- 2 teaspoons fresh parsley

- ¼ teaspoon thyme

- ⅛ teaspoon pepper

- 2 cups water

Directions:

1. In a medium saucepan, heat up the coconut oil.

2. Once heated, add the onion and cook until it is translucent.

3. Add the carrots, zucchini, parsley, thyme and pepper to the saucepan.

4. Cover and cook over low heat until the vegetables are tender—approximately 10 minutes.

5. Add the water and bring to a boil.

6. Reduce the heat to medium and cook until vegetables are soft—approximately 20 minutes. Once you've finished cooking the vegetables, remove the pot from the heat and allow it to cool slightly.

7. Remove ½ cup of soup from the pan and put it aside.

8. Pour the remaining soup into a blender and process at a low speed until you've reached a smooth consistency.

9. Combine the pureed mixture and the reserved soup into a saucepan and cook, stirring constantly until it is hot.

10. Serve and enjoy.

Note: If you prefer to leave your vegetables whole, just skip the blender step.

Chicken Chowder

Ingredients:

- 4 cups chicken, cubed

- 6 cups water

- 1 large chopped onion, divided in half

- 2 stalks celery, chopped, divided in half

- 1 cup chopped carrot, divided in half

- 6 large cloves garlic, finely chopped, divided in half

- ¼ cup chopped parsley, divided in half

- ½ teaspoon black pepper—more if desired

- 3 cups chicken stock

- 2 tablespoons olive oil

- 2 tablespoons coconut flour

- ½ cup coconut milk

- Salt to your liking

Directions:

1. Place the chicken, water, half of the onion, half of the celery, half of the carrot, half of the garlic, parsley, and black pepper in a small stockpot.

2. Bring the mixture to a boil.

3. Now reduce the heat, cover and let simmer for 45 minutes to 1 hour.

4. Strain the broth into another pot through a colander.

5. Discard the cooked vegetables.

6. Add the chicken stock to the pot and set aside.

7. In the large stockpot, heat the oil over medium heat.

8. Add the flour and the remaining onion, celery, carrot, garlic, and parsley and stir constantly until the onions are fragrant and translucent—approximately 5–6 minutes.

9. Whisking constantly, add the flour and cook for about 1 minute.

10. Now whisk in the chicken broth, making sure to stir constantly to avoid any clumping.

11. Bring the mixture to a boil and cook until tender— approximately 8 minutes more.

12. Add the cooked chicken and coconut milk and heat until warmed through.

13. Serve at desired temperature with additional salt and pepper to taste.

Lobster Bisque Paleo Style

Lobster Bisque is a soup that is smooth, creamy and so delicious. If you don't have enough time to make and enjoy this for lunch, be sure to put it on your dinner menu. It is wonderful!

Ingredients:

- 4 tablespoons butter or ghee

- 2 tablespoons scallions, diced

- 1 stalk celery, chopped

- 4 tablespoons coconut flour

- 2 cups PLUS 2 tablespoons coconut milk

- 1 tablespoon tomato paste

- 2 teaspoons paprika

- 1 teaspoon Old Bay Seasoning

- ⅛ teaspoon cayenne pepper

- 2–3 tablespoons chicken broth

- 10 ounces cooked, coarsely chopped lobster meat, drained well

- Salt and pepper to taste

Directions:

1. Melt butter in a saucepan over medium low heat.

2. Add the scallions and celery and cook for about 3 minutes until the vegetables begin to soften.

3. Add the coconut flour and blend into the vegetables.

4. Cook over medium heat for about 3 minutes, stirring frequently.

5. Slowly pour the coconut milk into the vegetable mixture and stir until blended.

6. Now stir in the tomato paste.

7. Cook over medium-low heat for about 5 minutes or until the bisque begins to thicken.

8. Add the paprika, Old Bay Seasoning, cayenne, and broth.

9. Stir to blend.

10. Add the cooked lobster meat.

11. Salt and pepper to taste.

12. Simmer the bisque over low heat for about 5 more minutes until heated through.

13. Do not boil!

Now savor every bite and enjoy!

Fast & Fresh Tomato Basil Soup

Ingredients:

- 3 large tomatoes, peeled and chopped

- 1 onion, chopped

- 4 garlic cloves, minced

- ½ teaspoon oregano

- ⅛ teaspoon marjoram

- ¼ cup fresh basil, coarsely chopped

- 2 cups chicken stock

- Salt and pepper to taste

Directions:

1. Place prepared tomatoes, onions, garlic, oregano, marjoram, and basil into a medium-sized saucepan. Add the chicken stock and bring to a boil.

2. Reduce the heat and simmer for approximately 20 minutes.

3. Cool for 10 minutes.

4. Pour the soup into a blender in small batches and run on high for a smooth consistency.

5. Repeat for each batch.

6. Each time, pour the soup back into another saucepan and reheat briefly before serving.

7. Garnish with fresh basil if desired.

Quick Chicken & Veggie Soup

Ingredients:

-   1 rotisserie chicken, meat removed and shredded

-   2 ribs of celery, chopped

-   ½ red onion, finely chopped

-   4 large carrots, thinly sliced

-   ½ large butternut squash, peeled and cubed

-   2 teaspoons minced garlic

-   1 teaspoon basil

-   1 teaspoon oregano

-   1 tablespoon balsamic vinegar

- Salt and pepper, to taste

- Fresh cold water

- A few sprigs of freshly chopped parsley

Directions:

1. Add shredded chicken, celery, onion, carrots, squash, garlic, basil, oregano, vinegar, salt and pepper to a large pot on the stove.

2. Pour fresh cold water over the chicken and veggies until submerged.

3. Place the lid on the pot and cook on high until the squash begins to soften—approximately 20 minutes.

4. Stir and serve with a sprinkling of fresh chopped parsley.

WRAPS

Lettuce Wraps

Ingredients:

- 1 avocado

- 1 chicken breast, cooked and cubed

- 2 tomatoes, chopped

- ¼ onion, chopped

- ½ bell pepper, chopped

- 1 clove garlic, minced

- 1 sprig fresh cilantro, minced

- Juice from 1 lime

- 4 large lettuce leaves

Directions:

1. Mash the avocado until it has a smooth texture that is spreadable.

2. To the avocado, add the chicken, tomatoes, onion, bell pepper, garlic, cilantro, and lime juice.

3. Mix well.

4. Place your desired amount of the mixture onto each lettuce leaf and wrap it up like a burrito.

Chicken Fajitas

Ingredients:

- 3 pounds chicken breast meat, cut into strips

- 3 bell peppers

- 3 onions, sliced

- 2 tablespoons oregano

- 2 tablespoons chili powder

- 2 tablespoons cumin

- 2 tablespoons coriander

- 6 garlic cloves, chopped

- Juice of 5 lemons

- 4 tablespoons coconut oil

- Butter lettuce leaves for the fajitas

- Almond slices for garnish

- Favorite toppings

Directions:

1. In a large bowl, combine the chicken, bell peppers, onions, oregano, chili powder, cumin, coriander, garlic and lemon juice into a bowl and mix well.

2. Allow the mixture to marinate in the refrigerator for 4 hours.

3. When you are ready to cook, place the coconut oil into a large skillet and melt over medium heat.

4. Cook the entire mixture until the chicken is cooked thoroughly and the onion and bell pepper are soft.

5. Remove the mixture from the heat and place into a large bowl.

6. Now place the desired amount of mixture into a lettuce leaf, top with almond slices and your favorite toppings, and enjoy.

No Mayo Egg Salad Wrap

Ingredients:

-   8 hard-boiled eggs

-   1 avocado, peeled with pit removed

-   ½ teaspoon dry mustard

-   2 tablespoons apple cider vinegar

-   ½ teaspoon sea salt

-   Whole lettuce leaves (romaine and butter lettuce work well)

Directions:

1. Take your hard-boiled eggs and separate the yolks from the whites.

2. Place the yolks, avocado, dry mustard, vinegar and salt in a large bowl and mash and mix until smooth.

3. Take the egg whites and chop them.

4. Now fold the egg whites and the salt into the mashed mixture.

5. Place desired amount into the lettuce leaves.

6. Serve immediately.

Spicy Tuna Salad Wrap

Ingredients:

- 24 ounces canned tuna (or wild-caught salmon)

- 1 tablespoon Paleolithic mayo (p. 16)

- ⅓ cup chopped and seeded jalapeno pepper

- ⅓ teaspoon onion powder

- ⅓ cup onion, chopped

- 15 to 20 baby carrots, cut in half

- ½ teaspoon sea salt

- ¼ cup salsa

- 8 ounce can tomato paste

Directions:

1. Combine all the ingredients in a medium bowl and mix well.

2. Enjoy this salad mixture wrapped in lettuce leaves or enjoy it with apple slices or celery.

Steak & Salsa Wrap

Ingredients:

- 1 serving of cooked skirt steak

- 1 tomato, chopped

- 1 avocado, peeled, pitted and cubed

- 1 teaspoon sea salt

- Juice from ½ lime

- 1 tablespoon apple cider vinegar

- 1 tablespoon olive oil

- Romaine or leafy lettuce for wraps

- Favorite salsa

Directions:

1. Place your lettuce leaf on a plate and place the skirt steak on top.

2. Put the tomato and avocado into a bowl.

3. In a small separate bowl, combine the salt, lime juice, vinegar, and oil until mixed well.

4. Pour the liquid mixture over the tomato and avocado and mix gently.

5. Top the steak with the mixture and add your favorite salsa.

Asian Lettuce Wraps

Ingredients

- 1 tablespoon macadamia nut oil

- ½ red onion, chopped

- 3 garlic cloves, minced

- 1½ teaspoon ginger, minced

- 1 pound ground beef

- 1 tablespoon coconut aminos

- If desired, you can add chopped veggies like zucchini, tomato, shredded carrots, sliced mushrooms

- Lettuce leaves or raw cabbage leaves for the wraps

- Cilantro to garnish

Directions:

1. In a large frying pan, put the oil and heat over a medium setting.

2. Once heated, add the onion and cook until translucent.

3. Add the garlic and ginger and cook for another minute or two.

4. Add the ground beef and cook until browned.

5. Once browned, add the aminos and stir to blend.

6. Place any chopped vegetables you would like to add into the pan and cook for a few minutes.

7. Remove from the heat and place desired amount onto a lettuce or cabbage leaf.

8. Garnish with nuts, cilantro, etc. and wrap.

Basic Paleo Wraps

Ingredients:

- 2 eggs

- 1 tablespoon coconut flour

- 3 tablespoons olive or coconut oil

- Salt to taste

- 3 tablespoons water

Directions:

1. Begin by whisking the eggs really well in a small bowl.

2. Process the coconut flour through a sifter.

3. Now add the flour to the whipped eggs, along with the olive oil and salt.

4. Mix well and whisk the mixture for one minute.

5. The mixture should be pourable like a pancake batter. If too thick to pour, add one tablespoon of water at a time until desired consistency is reached.

6. Heat a large frying pan with enough olive oil to cover the bottom.

7. Once the oil is heated, pour enough batter into the pan to make the size wrap you want.

8. Cook on medium heat for 3 to 4 minutes.

9. Flip to the other side and brown.

10. Drain and allow to cool.

11. Fill with your favorite filling.

QUICK BITES

Scallops & Sautéed Veggies

Ingredients:

- ½ red onion, thinly sliced

- 6 slices of thick nitrite/nitrate-free bacon (optional)

- 3 garlic cloves, minced

- 1 pound fresh snap peas

- 3 tablespoons flat leaf parsley, finely diced

- Juice from ½ a lemon

- ½ teaspoon dried thyme

- Salt and pepper to taste

- 2 tablespoons coconut oil

- 1 pound sea scallops, defrosted

- ½ cup chicken broth

Directions:

1. In a frying pan, sauté the onions and bacon for 4 minutes.

2. Add the garlic and snap peas and sauté for another 2 minutes.

3. Add the parsley, lemon juice, thyme, salt and pepper and cook for another minute.

60

4. Remove the veggie mixture from the pan and set aside.

5. Add the coconut oil to the skillet and heat over medium high heat.

6. Make sure your scallops are entirely defrosted and patted dry with paper towels.

7. Sprinkle the scallops with a bit of salt and pepper and sear the scallops for 1 minute on each side (they should be nice and brown).

8. Add the veggie mixture on top of the scallops, pour the chicken broth over the scallops and gently stir.

9. Bring to a boil and simmer for another minute or two. The scallops should be tender and cooked all the way through. Do not overcook scallops or their texture will become rubbery.

Chicken Salad-Stuffed Tomatoes

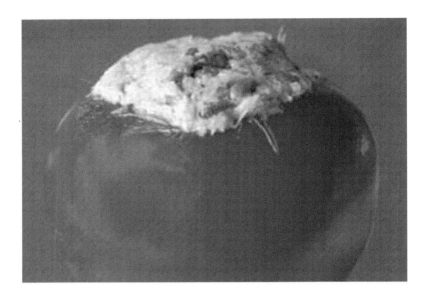

Ingredients:

- 6 large tomatoes

- 18 ounces of canned chicken, drained and crumbled

- 1 cup flat-leaf parsley leaves, chopped

- Zest of 1 lemon

- ¼ cup fresh lemon juice

- 1 tablespoon olive oil

- ¼ teaspoon black pepper

Directions:

1. Begin by hollowing out each tomato. Remove the stem end and scoop out the seeds and pulp, being careful not to pierce the skin.

2. Add the canned chicken, parsley, lemon zest, juice, oil and pepper to a bowl and mix thoroughly.

3. Carefully spoon the mixture into the hollowed-out tomatoes.

4. Yummy and pretty!

Eggplant Bruschetta

Ingredients:

- 7 ripe plum tomatoes

- 2 teaspoons apple cider vinegar

- 1 large eggplant

- 2 large eggs

- 2 cloves garlic, minced

- 8 fresh basil leaves, chopped

- 1 teaspoon paprika

- 1 teaspoon garlic powder

- ½ teaspoon sea salt

- ½ teaspoon black pepper

- ½ teaspoon dried thyme

- 1 teaspoon chipotle powder (optional)

- 1 cup almond flour

- 1 tablespoon olive oil

Directions:

1. Preheat your oven to 375 degrees F.

2. Place a pot on your stovetop that will allow your tomatoes to fit into it all at once

3. Fill the pot about ¾ full of water

4. Bring the water to a boil

5. Parboil the tomatoes for one minute in boiling water that has just been removed from the burner.

6. Drain.

7. Using a sharp small knife, remove the skins of the tomatoes.

8. Once the tomatoes are peeled, cut them in halves or quarters and remove the seeds and juice from their centers.

9. Also cut out and discard the stem area.

10. In a separate bowl, mix the tomatoes with the vinegar and set aside.

11. Slice the eggplant into 8 round slices, each about ½ inch thick.

12. Trim the skin, maintaining the round shape of the slices.

13. In a small bowl, whisk the eggs.

14. Mix dry ingredients and almond flour together and set aside in a separate small bowl.

15. Grease a large baking sheet or pizza pan with olive oil.

16. Dip the eggplant slices one at a time into the egg and then into the almond flour.

17. One by one, place the coated slices in a single layer on the prepared baking sheet or pizza pan greased with the olive oil.

18. Top the slices with the tomato topping.

19. Bake in the preheated oven approximately 15 minutes.

20. Now change the oven setting to broil and continue cooking 3 to 5 minutes.

21. Check the slices frequently during broiling to avoid burning.

22. Remove from the oven when you are pleased with the brownness of your topping.

Baltimore Crab Cakes

Ingredients:

- 1 pound crab meat

- 2 tablespoons coconut flour (or enough to make the mixture stick together)

- 1 egg

- ¼ cup minced fresh parsley

- 1 teaspoon crushed garlic

- ¼ cup Paleolithic mayonnaise (p. 16)

- 2 tablespoons spicy mustard

- Salt and pepper to taste

- ⅛ teaspoon of chipotle powder

- 3–4 tablespoons coconut oil

Directions:

1. If using the canned crab, make sure to crumble the crab with your hands into a large mixing bowl and pick out any shells you might find.

2. Mix the crab with the coconut flour, egg, parsley, garlic, mayo, mustard, salt, pepper, and chipotle powder.

3. In a large skillet, heat the coconut oil over medium heat for about 1 minute.

4. Form the crab cake mixture into palm-sized patties and fry for 2–3 minutes on each side or until they are golden brown.

They are amazing!

Crabby Mushrooms

Ingredients:

- 10 ounce package frozen spinach, thawed

- 1½ pounds Portabella mushrooms

- 2 tablespoons coconut oil

- ¼ cup onions, chopped

- 2 garlic cloves, minced

- ¼ cup chicken broth

- 1 tablespoon lemon juice

- ½ teaspoon dried basil

- ¼ teaspoon ground ginger

- ½ teaspoon dried oregano

- 12 ounces cooked crabmeat

Directions:

1. Preheat your oven to 425 degrees F.

2. Begin by squeezing as much of the excess liquid from your thawed spinach as you can.

3. Remove the stems and some of the inside flesh of the mushroom with a spoon.

4. Chop some of the stems to make enough for 2 cups.

5. In a large skillet, heat up the coconut oil over medium heat.

6. Once heated, put the chopped mushroom stems, onion, garlic, broth, and lemon juice into the pan.

7. Cook until the onion is tender.

8. Now add the spinach and cook until the liquid is evaporated.

9. Stir in the basil, ginger and oregano into the spinach.

10. Now add the crabmeat and mix gently.

11. Spoon the crab mixture into the mushroom tops.

12. Place the stuffed mushroom tops onto a lightly greased baking dish.

13. Bake for 10 to 15 minutes until the mushrooms are tender.

14. Remove from the oven and serve.

If you can't find Portabella mushrooms, just get some big button mushrooms and stuff them.

Apple Coleslaw

Ingredients:

- 2 cups packaged coleslaw mix (bag of chopped cabbage found in the produce section) OR shred your own cabbage

- 2 unpeeled tart apples, chopped

- ½ cup finely chopped celery

- ½ cup apple cider vinegar

- 2 tablespoons raw honey (optional)

- 1 tablespoon olive oil

Directions:

1. In a bowl, combine the coleslaw mix, apples, and celery.

2. In a separate smaller bowl, whisk together the vinegar, honey, and olive oil.

3. Now pour the dressing over the coleslaw and toss together to coat the slaw.

4. Enjoy.

Apricot and Coconut Nut Bars

Ingredients

- 1 cup slivered almonds

- 1 cup pecans

- ½ cup almond flour

- ½ cup coconut oil

- ½ cup almond butter

- ¼ cup raw honey

- 2 teaspoons pure vanilla extract

- ½ teaspoon sea salt

- 1 cup of dried apricots, chopped into small pieces

- ¼ to ½ cup of shredded unsweetened coconut

- Parchment paper

Directions

1. Place the slivered almonds and pecans on a cookie sheet and toast in a 350 degree oven for 8 to 10 minutes.

2. Now place the toasted nuts into a food processor and pulse until they are coarse.

3. Remove from the food processor and place in a medium bowl along with the almond flour and mix together.

4. In a microwaveable bowl, warm the coconut oil and the almond butter for about 20 seconds in the microwave until it has a fluid consistency when stirred.

5. Stir in the honey, vanilla and salt into the almond butter mixture.

6. Combine the flour mixture with the liquid almond butter mixture thoroughly.

7. Add the apricot pieces and coconut and combine well OR you could use the coconut to coat the top of the bars.

8. Lay parchment paper down in an 8 × 8 inch baking pan.

9. Pat the mixture into the prepared pan with your fingers, making sure it is packed down well.

10. Place in the refrigerator to harden or freezer for at least 1 hour.

11. Cut into pieces and serve.

Index of Recipes' Main Ingredients

In this index, I have listed some of the main ingredients used in the recipes. If you are new to the Paleo lifestyle, this index will show you some of the ingredients that are often used in recipes. If you have been eating Paleo for quite awhile, some of the ingredients listed in this index will be items you always keep on hand.

Spices and other condiments are not usually referenced here; however, ones like coconut oil and chicken broth are—mostly to help newbies get used to seeing these ingredients. Seldom used items like crabmeat and bacon are mentioned so you can easily find a recipe that uses these ingredients that you may have on hand and others you want to use up.

Under each item, I have included the page number to the recipe where that ingredient is used.

~ butternut squash

Quick Chicken & Veggie Soup 40

~ cabbage

Asian Lobster Salad 18

Cabbage and Beef Soup 27

~ carrots

Hearty Sautéed Peach Salad 9

Cabbage and Beef Soup 27

Easy Vegetable Soup 31

Chicken Chowder 33

Quick Chicken & Veggie Soup 40

Spicy Tuna Salad Wrap 50

~ celery

Fruity Salad with Chicken 15

Cabbage and Beef Soup 27

Chicken Chowder 33

Lobster Bisque Paleo Style 35

Quick Chicken & Veggie Soup 40

Apple Coleslaw 72

~ cheese, aged cheddar

Poached Egg Salad 22

~ chicken, broth

Asian Lobster Salad 18

Sweet Potato Soup 29

79

Apricot and Coconut Nut Bars 74

~ jalapeno pepper
Spicy Tuna Salad Wrap 50

~ lemons and lemon juice, fresh
Fruity Salad with Chicken 15

Warm Shrimp Salad 20

Poached Egg Salad 22

Quick Chicken & Veggie Soup 40

Chicken Fajitas 47

Scallops & Sautéed Veggies 60

Chicken Salad-Stuffed Tomatoes 62

Crabby Mushrooms 69

~ lettuce leaves
Lettuce Wraps 45

Chicken Fajitas 47

No Mayo Egg Salad Wrap 49

~ lime juice
Lettuce Wraps 45

Steak & Salsa Wrap 52

~ lobster, cooked
Asian Lobster Salad 18

Lobster Bisque Paleo Style 35

~ mayo, Paleo
Fruity Salad with Chicken 15

Spicy Tuna Salad Wrap 50

Quick Chicken & Veggie Soup	40
Scallops & Sautéed Veggies	60
Chicken Salad-Stuffed Tomatoes	62
Baltimore Crab Cakes	67

~ peaches, fresh or frozen

Hearty Sautéed Peach Salad	9

~ pecans

Fruity Salad with Chicken	15
Apricot and Coconut Nut Bars	74

~ romaine lettuce

Hearty Sautéed Peach Salad	9
Grilled Taco Salad	13

~ scallions

Lobster Bisque Paleo Style	35

~ scallops

Scallops & Sautéed Veggies	60

~ sesame oil

Asian Lobster Salad	18

~ sesame seeds

Warm Shrimp Salad	20

~ shrimp, raw

Warm Shrimp Salad	20

~ snap peas

Warm Shrimp Salad	20
Scallops & Sautéed Veggies	60

~ spinach, frozen

Crabby Mushrooms	69

~ steak, skirt

Grilled Taco Salad	13
Steak & Salsa Wrap	52

~ sweet bell peppers

Grilled Taco Salad	13
Asian Lobster Salad	18
Quick Chicken & Veggie Soup	40
Lettuce Wraps	45
Chicken Fajitas	47

~ sweet potatoes

Sweet Potato Soup	29

~ tomatoes, diced

Cabbage and Beef Soup	27

~ tomato, fresh

Grilled Taco Salad	13
Fast & Fresh Tomato Basil Soup	38
Lettuce Wraps	45
Steak & Salsa Wrap	52
Chicken Salad-Stuffed Tomatoes	62

Eggplant Bruschetta   64

~ tomato juice

Cabbage and Beef Soup   27
Asian Lettuce Wraps   54

~ tomato paste

Lobster Bisque Paleo Style   35
Spicy Tuna Salad Wrap   50

~ tuna, canned

Spicy Tuna Salad Wrap   50

~ water chestnuts

Asian Lobster Salad   18

~ zucchini

Warm Shrimp Salad   20
Easy Vegetable Soup   31

Additional Resources

Gluten-Free Slow Cooker: Easy Recipes for a Gluten Free Diet

Paleo Slow Cooker Soups and Stews: Healthy Family Gluten-Free Recipes

Paleo Slow Cooker: Simple and Healthy Gluten-Free Recipes

Going Paleo: A Quick Start Guide for a Gluten-Free Diet

4 Weeks of Fabulous Paleolithic Breakfasts

4 MORE Weeks of Fabulous Paleolithic Breakfasts

4 Weeks of Fabulous Paleolithic Dinners

The Ultimate Paleolithic Collection

About the Author

Amelia Simons is a food enthusiast, wife, and mother of five. Frustrated with traditional dieting advice, she stumbled upon the Paleolithic lifestyle of eating and has never looked back. Without bothering to count calories or stress about endless hours of exercise, eating the Paleolithic way enabled Amelia and her husband to effortlessly drop pounds and lower their cholesterol.

Amelia now enjoys sharing the Paleolithic philosophy with friends and readers and finding new ways to turn favorite recipes into healthy alternatives.

Acknowledgements

I would like to thank the following artists for sharing their photos:

- SirNico

- jeffreyw

Made in the USA
Middletown, DE
16 May 2022